D0849795

THE WORLD OF DRAGONS

DRAGONS IN MYTHOLOGY

BY MATT DOEDEN

READING CONSULTANT:
BARBARA J. FOX
PROFESSOR EMERITA
NORTH CAROLINA STATE UNIVERSITY

CAPSTONE PRESS
a capstone imprint

Blazers Books are published by Capstone Press,
1710 Roe Crest Drive, North Mankato, Minnesota 56003
www.capstonepub.com

Library of Congress Cataloging-in-Publication Data
Doeden, Matt.
Dragons in mythology / by Matt Doeden.
pages cm—(Blazers. The world of the dragons)
Includes bibliographical references and index.
Summary: "Describes popular dragon legends and myths from around
the world"—Provided by publisher.
ISBN 978-1-62065-143-8 (library binding)
ISBN 978-1-4765-1375-1 (ebook PDF)
1. Dragons—Juvenile literature. I. Title.
GR830.D7D645 2013
398.24'54—dc23   2012033237

Editorial Credits
Aaron Sautter, editor; Kyle Grenz, designer; Eric Gohl, media researcher;
Jennifer Walker, production specialist

Photo Credits
Capstone: Jonathan Mayer, 12–13, 24, Richard Pellegrino, 4–5, 6–7, 9, 10–11, 15, 20–21; Dreamstime:
Claudiodivizia, 16–17; Mary Evans Picture Library: Sammlung Rauch/INTERFOTO, 18; Newscom:
Album/Warner Bros., 28–29; Shutterstock: 123Nelson, 27, Linda Bucklin, cover, Stephen Rudolph,
22–23, Unholy Vault Designs, cover (background), 1

Design Elements
Shutterstock

Printed in the United States of America in Brainerd, Minnesota.
092012   006938BANGS13

TABLE of CONTENTS

BEOWULF FIGHTS
THE DRAGON. 4

HISTORY OF
DRAGON MYTHS. 8

DRAGONS
OF THE WEST. 12

DRAGONS OF
THE EAST. 20

TODAY'S DRAGONS 26

GLOSSARY. 30

READ MORE 31

INTERNET SITES. 31

INDEX 32

BEOWULF FIGHTS THE DRAGON

The Kingdom of Geatland was
in trouble. A fire-breathing dragon
was burning farms and villages. King
Beowulf marched to the dragon's **lair**.
But the dragon was waiting. Most of
the king's men ran away in fear.

lair—a place where a wild animal lives and sleeps

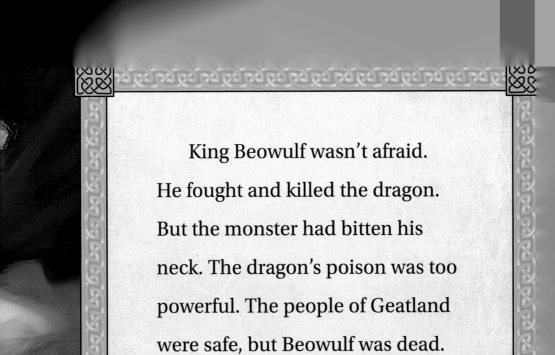

King Beowulf wasn't afraid. He fought and killed the dragon. But the monster had bitten his neck. The dragon's poison was too powerful. The people of Geatland were safe, but Beowulf was dead.

DRAGON FACT

The story of Beowulf was written more than 800 years ago.

HISTORY OF DRAGON MYTHS

Dragon **myths** have been told for thousands of years. Ancient people often told wild stories about crocodiles and other scary creatures. Over time the creatures in the stories may have become fierce fire-breathing dragons.

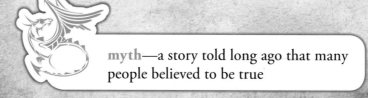

myth—a story told long ago that many people believed to be true

DRAGON FACT

Stories about powerful dragons come from all over the world.

People long ago might have thought lightning was a dragon breathing fire in the sky.

Ancient people may also have discovered old dinosaur bones. But they would not have known what kind of bones they were. These people may have created stories about dragons to explain the large bones.

DRAGONS
OF THE WEST

In Western dragon stories, dragons are often terrifying monsters. They burn villages with their fiery breath. They often kidnap people and steal treasure. Heroes usually kill the dragons to save people.

Saint George and the Dragon

In one famous story, a town gave a dragon all of its sheep. But the dragon also demanded the town's children. The people started a **lottery** to decide which children to **sacrifice**.

lottery—a way of randomly choosing someone
sacrifice—to give something up for the good of others

The king's daughter was soon chosen. She was left near the dragon's lair. But Saint George rode to the rescue. He killed the monster with his lance. The town was safe.

DRAGON FACT

To honor Saint George, the king built a church on the spot where the dragon was killed.

lance—a long spear used by soldiers on horseback

THE LEGEND OF SIGURD

One day Sigurd was asked to kill the mighty dragon Fafnir. Sigurd hid in a hole near Fafnir's lair. As the dragon passed over him, Sigurd thrust his sword into Fafnir's belly. Sigurd then kept Fafnir's treasure as his reward.

Fafnir's magical blood gave Sigurd special powers. He became stronger and faster. His skin became as tough as a dragon's. Sigurd could even understand the speech of birds.

19

DRAGONS OF THE EAST

Dragons in Eastern stories aren't mean monsters. Eastern dragons are respected for their power and **wisdom**. In many stories these dragons are helpful and bring good luck.

wisdom—knowledge, experience, and good judgment

THE FOUR DRAGONS

One Chinese story tells about a terrible **drought**. Four helpful dragons scooped up ocean water. They sprayed it onto people's **crops** as rain. The dragons then became rivers so the people would always have water for their crops.

drought—a long period of weather with little or no rainfall

crop—a plant farmers grow in large amounts, usually for food

DRAGON FACT

The four main rivers of China are the Black River, the Yangtze (Long) River, the Pearl River, and the Yellow River. These rivers are named after the four helpful dragons.

Yangtze (Long) River

THE DRAGON'S PEARL

Another Chinese story tells of a boy named Xiao who found a magic pearl. The pearl made food grow quickly. Xiao swallowed the pearl one day to keep it safe from hungry thieves. But the pearl turned Xiao into a dragon. As a dragon, he made sure the village's crops always grew well.

DRAGON FACT

Eastern dragons are often shown carrying large magic pearls. The pearls stand for wisdom.

TODAY'S DRAGONS

Eastern dragons are still **honored** in some countries. Chinese New Year festivals often include handmade dragons in parades. The Year of the Dragon happens every 12 years on the Chinese calendar. People born in these years are said to have good luck.

honor—to give praise or show respect

Chinese New Year parade

Today dragons come to life in many books and comics. Video games and movies also feature fierce dragons. Dragons are just **fantasy** creatures, but they live on in stories around the world.

fantasy—a story with made-up creatures, places, and events

In *The Hobbit* by J.R.R. Tolkien, several people join together to defeat the fearsome dragon Smaug.

GLOSSARY

crop (KROP)—a plant farmers grow in large amounts, usually for food

drought (DROUT)—a long period of weather with little or no rainfall

fantasy (FAN-tuh-see)—a story with made-up creatures, places, and events

honor (ON-ur)—to give praise or show respect

lair (LAIR)—a place where a wild animal lives and sleeps

lance (LANSS)—a long spear used by soldiers on horseback

lottery (LOT-ur-ee)—a way of randomly choosing someone

myth (MITH)—a story told long ago that many people believed to be true

sacrifice (SAK-ruh-fysse)—to give something up for the good of others

wisdom (WIZ-duhm)—knowledge, experience, and good judgment

Read More

Buillain, Charlotte. *Dragons.* Mythical Creatures. Chicago: Raintree, 2011.

Caldwell, S.A. *Dragonworld.* Philadelphia: RP Kids, 2011.

Malam, John. *Dragons.* Mythologies. Irvine, Calif.: QEB Pub., 2009.

Internet Sites

FactHound offers a safe, fun way to find Internet sites related to this book. All of the sites on FactHound have been researched by our staff.

Here's all you do:

Visit *www.facthound.com*

Type in this code: 9781620651438

Check out projects, games and lots more at
www.capstonekids.com

INDEX

breathing fire, 8, 11, 13

Chinese New Year, 26
Chinese rivers, 22, 23

dinosaur bones, 11
dragon myths
    creation of, 8, 11
    Eastern myths, 20
    Western myths, 13

famous dragons
    Fafnir, 19
    Smaug, 29

helpful dragons, 20, 22, 23, 25
heroes, 13
    Beowulf, 4, 7
    Saint George, 14, 17
    Sigurd, 19

lairs, 4, 19

magical powers, 19
magic pearls, 25
modern dragon stories
    books, 28
    comic books, 28
    Hobbit, The, 29
    movies, 28
    video games, 28

treasure, 13, 19

Year of the Dragon, 26